I0475545

30 Maximum Conversion Rate Tips

"Increase Your Sales Copy's Conversion Rate By Making Minimum Changes That Deliver Maximum Impact!"

**from the library of the
New Thrive Learning Institute**

Get Related Materials

from Our Free Library

Instant Access – Join Here

Click or type into your browser:

http://livesensical.com/go/byob/

LEGAL NOTICE

Table of Contents

Copywriting Today

The use of sales letters had been around for as long as direct response marketing have been practiced in the conventional "brick and mortar" world.

And ever since the Berlin wall came down and the World Wide Web came up, it did not take long for people from business backgrounds to tap into the growing world of E-Commerce.

And it certainly didn't take long for direct response marketers to carry their offline practice into the online world.

Thus, you see the practice of one-page-long sales letters being used widely today by businesses of various sizes to sell and push their products and/or services into the Internet marketplace.

This is the case, because sales letters in this fashion have been proven to be all time-tested. As you probably know by now, sales letters are really just one LONG page with one person in mind: to help sell the product to the prospect.

It's like an electronic salesperson on your behalf, and it certainly beats having you to prospect and sell to someone else face-to-face or gamble on sending out hard copy mails (that can span 5-20 pages long when printed) and face the chance of not covering your investment on printing back.

A sales letter is considered to produce a good decent conversion rate at 2 to 4 percent. You are doing better if your sales letter produces above 4 percent. Some marketers reportedly produce 6% and some as high as 20-30% to cold prospects!

Believe it or not, online sales letter consists of mainly the use of mostly words and then some images. And words are indeed powerful tools; you should consider them double-edged swords.

If used correctly, words can sell literally. If used improperly, not only would your sales letter suffer in conversion rate, it might just deliver the wrong message and the worse case scenario can be that of offending your prospects (besides not closing the sale).

I have a sneaky suspicion that your sales letters are currently not producing the kind of conversion rates you want. Or this is your first try at developing a life long asset or skill where marketing online is concerned.

Perhaps you want to seek all ways possible to offer your sales copies a boost without having to spend a fortune on expensive copywriters in the process because you don't have the deep pockets for it at the moment.

Regardless of your current needs, I trust that you will find this guide useful and that when you apply these tips into your sales copies, you will see substantial results in your conversion rates.

Read on and discover how tips you can use to MAXIMIZE your conversion rates by making

30 Maximum Conversion Rate Tips - 4

MINIMUM changes and additions to your current sales copies!

Headline & Sub-Headline

- Color your headline red.

The color "red" usually symbolizes urgency or importance. Alternatively, you can use "black" or text with "yellow highlight in the background" if "red" won't suit your sales copy's color theme.

However, it is advisable to use "red" as the color of your headline plus this color can be used with almost any theme color suitably.

- Your headline font must be larger than the standard font used for your sales letter.

The purpose of your headline is to grab your prospect's attention to read and qualify him or her. Thus it's important for your headline to stand out from the rest of your standard font.

Usually, the headline font is 1 or 2 times larger than your standard font.

- Imply a benefit or a summary of your offer in the headline.

And the benefit should often refer to your prospect, not YOU or someone else. Even if you are using another character in the headline, make absolutely sure that it ultimately has to do with your prospect and why or how it could benefit him or her.

Speaking of characters...

- Introduce a character in your headline.

It makes your sales copy more interesting to read and in many cases, relate it to your prospects. For example:

> *"Discover How A 24 Year Old Student Is Making THREE Times More In Income Than His University Professor On The Internet!"*

This headline is best aimed at young and the young at heart who wants to know how to make money online.

Or:

> *"How A 27 Year Old Unemployed Chap Broke Out Of Bankruptcy And Became*

Financially FREE... And How YOU Can Do It, Too!"

This headline is best aimed at people who are broke or bankrupt and how they can improve their financial status, regardless of how old they are.

Depending on the nature of your product or service, the more you can relate it to the majority of your prospects, the higher the chances you can hook your readers to read your sales letter, and then hopefully purchase from you.

- Your sub headline serves as a hook to make your readers continue reading.

The sub headline goes on to explore other benefits for your reader to continue reading, which are not shared in the headline.

The sub headline is generally smaller than the headline in font size (by 1), and is often differently colored, too. Black is a matching color for the sub headline. In short, you want to make your prospects feel that they owe it to themselves to read every line of your letter.

- Don't use too many words in the headline.

As a general rule of thumb, use in between 20 to 25 words for your headline, and 4-6 lines.

Don't make your headline too long to read otherwise your prospect would just get lazy immediately and leave your sales page without knowing the full benefit of your offer.

Opening of Your Sales Copy

Start your copy with a story.

Many average sales copies today are written in such a boring manner. You can immediately hook your prospect's interest by relating a fable or preferably a true story on your account.

Most importantly, the story must have to do with your offer later in the middle of your sales copy. Here's an example:

Once upon a time, there were three friends who have decided to take a short break from a long discussion. They agreed to row a boat to the middle of a lake and have an afternoon tea.

The three friends rented a boat and rowed to the middle of the lake. As they sat down to enjoy their tea, they realized that they had forgotten to bring the teapot. "I'll get the teapot," said the first friend, voluntarily. He stood up, put one leg over the side of the boat, and began to walk on the water to the shore and back to the boat with the teapot.

As they boiled the water, the realized that they had forgotten the tea leaves, too. They laughed at each other, and the second friend volunteered to take get the tea leaves. He put one leg over the side of the boat and walked on water. He returned shortly after getting the tea leaves by walking on water, too.

The three friends soon enjoy their afternoon tea on the boat, but it would be nicer if they had some tidbits. The third friend volunteered to get some tidbits from the shop rows by the shore, though he was somewhat reluctant to do so. He insisted so anyway.

He stood up like the other friends and put one leg over the side of the boat. He began to put his weight on his leg and... SPLASH! He sank and struggled to keep himself afloat. Seeing that he was drowning, the other two friends jumped in to rescue him.

As the third friend climbed into boat for safety, soaking wet, he asked, "How did you two manage to walk on water?" The two friends looked at each other and said, "*Oh, that's because we know where the rocks are.*"

Address an important or critical issue.

If your product is closely related to a very important or critical recent issue faced by majority of your prospects, there is no better case scenario than this (or niche marketing at its best as I'd like to call)!

For instance, if most of your prospects are currently facing a problem with rewriting Private Label articles and your product is an article rewriter software, then you can write your opening letter addressing the "article rewriting" problem, such as:

Most people today carelessly purchase the Private Label Rights to articles... that have already been sold and used by hundreds, maybe thousands.

And the result: plenty of Search Engine penalization, submission rejections from article directories and an army of riddling copycats.

Sure, one way is to rewrite the articles completely to be unique, but won't that waste your time? And if you're going to spend hours rewriting, won't it defeat the purpose of purchasing Private Label articles to help you save time?

Make safe assumptions about your prospect.

While some successful people adopt the "don't make assumptions" attitude, the truth is that you can still make some safe assumptions now and then... and people DO make assumptions now and then, whether they know it or not.

Here's another fact: people can be predictable.

This is proven in an informal study when a speaker asked the audience 3 simple questions. They didn't have to reply him just yet and they were instructed to only remember their answers.

The 3 questions he asked were:

1) Think of one number,

2) Think of a color, and

3) Think of a flower.

When the audience made their mind up in a flash, he went to ask, "For the first question, how many of you were thinking of '7'?" Easily more than 75% of the floor raised their hands up.

This was also the case when he asked if they were thinking of blue and rose for the subsequent questions. Overall, he guessed AT LEAST ONE answer correctly of the 3 questions... more than 75% of the time!

Amazing, isn't it?

While this was a mere study, it goes to show that people are predictable and as long as you understand the majority of your prospects and their needs, you would've qualified a big fraction of them!

For example:

I have a sneaky suspicion that you're on a tight budget and have less than a few hundreds to spend on your marketing and advertising campaign.

OR:

Chances are that you have failed in your past relationships or this is your first try at scoring a date with your dream girl.

Be sure to follow in by mentioning a problem your prospect is facing.

You want to qualify your prospect by telling him or her the problem he or she is facing.

And then, you want to make the problem "sound" BIGGER, as if it's a real big deal.

Remember! Be careful not to go overboard with exaggeration, but you want to make it really important that your prospect should tackle the problem a.s.a.p. (with your product or service, of course).

Don't forget to introduce yourself!

You don't have to make it super fanciful, though. A simple introduction would suffice. For example:

My name is John Doe and I have been designing graphics for a living since 1998.

The Middle Section of Your Sales Copy

- Introduce your solution through your product or service.

You may want to show your prospect some other alternatives before moving in with your own, but show them to be somewhat less viable than yours.

For instance:

Sure, you can attend a seminar but UNLESS you have the deep pockets, this option is well way out.

And guesswork? Forget it. You don't have the risk tolerance for more financial mistakes and no more time to waste!

So what's the best solution?

Introducing "Your Name Product Here"...

- Put all your benefits in bullet form.

There is no neater way than to highlight all the benefits of your product or service out in bullet form (spaced out in between) like:

- Insert benefit #1

- Insert benefit #2

- Insert benefit #3

Important! Don't confuse benefits with features. Features are what your product may appear and look like. Benefits are what the product can DO for your prospect's good.

For example:

Feature: The product comes in PDF format.

Benefit: You can download the product instantly and not have to wait for 6 weeks of delivery!

Feature: The E-Book is 40 pages long.

Benefits: My manual doesn't carry fluffs, hypes and "beat around the bush" material. You get strictly all of what you need to know from my manual and I promise you all your guesswork will be eliminated 40 pages later!

If you are running a membership site or the product has a lot of components to address, divide the benefits section into several easy-to-read portions.

You will do well to table the components and sections of the benefits accordingly. For instance:

Component 1:

The Resell Rights Library

Every month, you receive 10 brand new products with Master Resell Rights. I guarantee you've never seen them before, because we are taking the liberty of producing the products straight from our hot hard drive! And you can resell these products at any price you wish and keep 100% of the sales... no profit sharing involved!

Component 2:

Sales Letters & Graphics Pack

With each of the new products, you also receive a professionally written sales letter complete with mini site graphics to help you sell the products for you!

Give only hints in the benefits, but don't give the secret away!

Because when you give the secrets or the contents of your product away, there really is no point in prospects buying your product... because all the core information are readily available in your sales letter!

Also, don't make it easy for people to guess your contents or secrets.

For example:

Discover the one little trick you can use to maximize your conversion rate... just by adding this ONE word to your headline!

OR

How to use G_____ to build your mailing list at ZERO COST!

Stress more on "What's in it for your prospects" and don't be too much of yourself.

In other words, refrain from using too many "I"s and more of "YOU"s in your benefits. Generally, people don't like self-centered people (even if they are themselves).

Throwing in Endorsements &

Testimonials

- Use photos and/or URLs below the names of your testimonies.

Not only does it make your testimonials more believable (since mere text and names can be easily faked by just about anyone), the URLs make it possible for your prospects to possibly crosscheck with them.

Also, photos add a hidden message whereby you took some effort to get these people to endorse you and your product/service.

So make an effort to get not only the URLs but also photos where possible.

- If possible, add audio or video.

This would also add the "believability" factor to your testimonials. Also, it's easier for your customers to relate their happy experiences from benefiting from your product or service through their own personal touch i.e. voice or video.

- Present the testimonials in a nice yellow-shade box.

Light Yellow has been proven to be the ideal color for testimonials in boxes. Alternatively, you can go for "gray" shade depending on your sales copy's color scheme.

- If you have a lot of testimonials, pepper them throughout your sales copy.

You can delegate the testimonials around the your sales copy in a convenient-reading format, with the best testimonial placed right below your sub headline.

The other testimonials can be peppered in ones, twos or threes below every component or before another sub headline in the body of the sales copy.

- If you have few testimonials, save them for below mid section.

If you have too few testimonials to pepper them throughout your sales copy, you will do well to save all or most of the testimonials in the below mid section where you prove your credibility by letting others "doing the talk" for you.

You may still want to save the best 1 or 2 testimonials and place them somewhere below the sub headline, to encourage your prospects to read on.

- Make sure your testimonials are results-oriented.

In short, your testimonials shouldn't be about "Wow John! You're great!" (If your name is really John, of course). It should be about what your product or service done to benefit the testimony.

Call to Action

If you are delivering a digital product such as E-Book, report, software, or script, remind your prospect that the delivery is instant.

For example:

The delivery process is automated and you can receive the manual instantly upon purchase. So, it doesn't matter even if it's 4:00AM in the morning so **purchase your copy right now** and you discover how you can tap into the planet's BIGGEST social networking site and bring your business to **greater heights**!

Avoid using the "until midnight" excuse.

This is primarily the case in Internet Marketing circles where most savvy marketers know it's really only a script at work. Unless you really meant that your product offer would be gone by midnight, you should refrain from using this tactic.

Because in ways more than one, it's pretty misleading even in pursuit of getting your prospects to act now. Evidently, your product would still be there the next day, being sold at the same price.

So use any other scarcity factors... but this!

Press your prospect to act on scarcity reasons.

You can say that you're limiting the number of copies of your product (and keep your word on it!).

And it has been proven that scarcity sells. People by nature like to have the privilege of owning so this is one factor you can really bang on to increase your conversion rate and sales.

For example:

Time-Based

This is NOT an open-ended offer. This sale runs for only 7 days. After the 7th day is past, this offer will expire and be removed forever!

Quantity Based

Only 100 copies will be sold. No more than that. Once the 100th copy leaves the shelf, this offer will not be made available again, EVER!

Use Fast Action Bonuses.

Nowadays, just offering bonuses just isn't enough an incentive especially if you're in a competitive niche. So you can add your edge by offering time sensitive bonuses.

Aside from your bonuses having to be perfect complimentary products to your primary offer, the fact that they are scarce encourages your prospect to act now and swap the Fast Action Bonuses and get rewarded more value for the same money purchased.

Tighten the offer with a long-term guarantee.

The longer your guarantee term, the better. Encourage your prospect to try your product out and test-drive it instead of being neutral or indifferent.

Here's an example:

Don't wonder. Don't think. Just try.

Also assure your prospect that you will be shouldering all the risk for him or her throughout the guarantee period.

I stake my reputation on my claims (in as bold as they may be), but I seriously hate to see you pass such a great deal that I'm willing to shoulder all the risks for you so you can try it out worry-free!

You may continue to go on and write:

You have my word that this is the big break through you're looking for.

And if it's not up to your satisfaction for any reason whatsoever, just drop me an email, delete the product off your hard drive, and I'll refund every cent of your purchase. No questions asked.

You have nothing to lose except a chance to try it out!

Use P.S.'s to summarize your offer or reveal hidden benefits.

Here are some things worth summarizing in your P.S. (or post-script), even though you don't have to cover all of them; some will do:

- You are shouldering the risk for your prospect through your Money Back Guarantee.

- It would be more expensive and costly in terms of money, time and effort (or all) if your prospect seeks other solutions or alternatives than yours.

- You can stress on the Fast Action Bonuses and how scarce they are that if your prospect doesn't act now, he or she will miss them out.

- If you have no other urgency factors, stress it out to your prospect on how valuable it is to him or her to tackle her current problems right NOW and not later with your offer.

- You can use the P.S. to reveal other hidden benefits not mentioned earlier in your sales letter. It could be an unannounced bonus, guarantee statement or a reward for acting immediately.

- You can choose to reveal even more praises and testimonials in effort to encourage your prospect to act now and become your customer.

All in all, P.S.es serve as good summaries and presses your prospect to act now by purchasing from your order link/button/form.

Tell your prospect that the price you're asking for is a bargain.

You can do this by comparing to other possibly higher cost solutions by your competitors (without naming names) or less effective alternatives.

For example:

Which one do you think is a smart thing to do? Invest $97.00 and find out all of what you need to know about making a killing in the stock market OR flushing thousands of dollars into shooting in the dark – and get killed in the process?

OR

For the first time ever, you can tap into the secrets of top marketers at the measly price of $47.00. Now why would you even pay $2,000 to attend a seminar to learn the same secrets I share with you in my audio course?

Bonus

Get Related Materials

from Our Free Library

Instant Access – Join Here

Click or type into your browser:

http://livesensical.com/go/byob/